Boundaries = Freedom

Boundaries = Freedom

How to Create Boundaries that Set You Free Without Feeling Guilty

Joseph Nguyen

AMARYLLIS

AMARYLLIS

An imprint of Manjul Publishing House Pvt. Ltd.
• C-16, Sector 3, Noida, Uttar Pradesh 201301, India
Website: www.manjulindia.com
Registered Office:
• 10, Nishat Colony, Bhopal 462 003 – India
Distribution Centres
Ahmedabad, Bengaluru, Bhopal, Chennai, Hyderabad,
Kolkata, Mumbai, Noida, Pune

Boundaries = Freedom: How to Create Boundaries that Set You Free Without Feeling Guilty by Joseph Nguyen.

Original English language edition published by
One Satori LLC Orlando, Florida USA. Arranged via
Licensor's Agent:DropCap Inc.

This edition first published in India in 2024

ISBN 978-93-5543-607-8

Printed and bound in India by Thomson Press (India) Ltd.

My Other Books

- Don't Believe Everything You Think: Why Your Thinking Is the Beginning & End of Suffering
- Beyond Thoughts: An Exploration of Who We Are Beyond Our Minds
- Healing Anxiety & Overthinking Journal & Workbook: Let Go of Anxiety, Overcome Fear, Find Peace & End Suffering
- The Couple's Connection Journal: 33 Questions to Create More Intimacy, Understanding & Love With Your Partner
- I also have courses on writing and creativity.
- You may find my work on my website at www.josephnguyen.org. My books can also be found on Amazon and many other online sites that sell books.

for all those on the journey of finding themselves again

Contents

"Have a heart soft enough to give love and mercy, but that is wise enough to know boundaries."

— Kayil Crow

Introduction

This book is a guide to help you find more peace, fulfillment, and joy.

Everything comes from nothing. For there to be a new creation, there must first be space. The same is true for our lives.

For us to have new experiences that transform us, we must first create space for them to possibly occur.

We cannot plant a new seed where a flower already exists.

The way for us to create space is by setting boundaries. Where there are boundaries, there is peace.

All possibilities, including a life we love, exist within the space we create within ourselves.

This book, as with all my books, is designed to be succinct and simple, created with the intention of evoking the wisdom within you in the fewest words possible.

Do not mistake its brevity for lack of potency.

It takes only one idea, one thought, one insight to change your life.

The words in this book are not *the* truth, but they help point you to **your** truth.

Knowledge informs. Truth transforms. Do not seek to be informed; seek to be *transformed*.

Chapter 1
A Life Without Boundaries

“Daring to set boundaries is about having the courage to love ourselves, even when we risk disappointing others.”

— Brené Brown

As soon as we are born, we are immediately thrown into a world where we're told what we should do, what we should think, how we should behave, whom we should spend time with, what we should wear, what job we should get, and what we should believe.

We grew up learning we should listen to everyone around us and are promised that if we do, we will have a joyful, peaceful, and fulfilling life filled with love — but how many of us actually feel this way?

The people in your life most likely mean well; they are simply doing the best they can with what they know, but this doesn't mean it is always helpful.

How often has listening to what others think we should do led us to create the life we want?

No one has lived your life, had the same experiences, and thinks or feels the way you do, so how can someone else possibly know what you want better than you do?

We constantly seek advice and answers from everyone else but ourselves.

We run in vicious circles, continuously overextending ourselves in the hopes of finally gaining the approval of others when all we desire is our approval of ourselves.

Yet we wonder why we feel overworked, stressed, anxious, and unfulfilled when we are supposedly "doing everything right" — according to everyone else's standards.

This is what it feels like to live a life without boundaries.

Society often teaches us to be accommodating, to put others before ourselves, and to sacrifice our own needs for others. But this is a form of self-betrayal. When we neglect our needs by not having boundaries, we lose touch with our inner self and become disconnected from our truth to the point where we no longer know who we are.

By constantly saying yes to everyone else we are inadvertently saying no to ourselves.

Creating a life full of love, happiness, and fulfillment begins by saying yes to yourself and no to things that no longer bring you those feelings.

This is not about going to the other end of the extremes and only saying no to others all the time. It is about restoring balance by giving yourself permission to say yes to yourself as much as you say yes to others because you understand that you matter as much as they do.

Your peace is an inside job. No one else can grant you this other than yourself.

Without boundaries, there is no space for what you want in your life.

Creating a life you love starts by taking back your life through putting boundaries in place to create space for what makes you feel alive and brings you joy.

"Love yourself enough to set boundaries. Your time and energy are precious, and you get to decide how you use them.

You teach people how to treat you by deciding what you will and won't accept."

— Anna Taylor

Chapter 2
Letting Go of the Guilt from Saying “No”

Once you realize that you do not need permission from anyone to choose a life of peace and joy, you are free.

Due to our conditioning, we primarily focus on the external world. We've been raised to believe that what other people think of us is more important than what we think about ourselves. As a result, much of our behaviors and actions are to earn the approval of others.

When we do this, the majority of our attention is directed toward the outer world; thus, our energy follows. If you feel exhausted, drained, and uninspired, this is because most of your energy is concentrated on the external world, leaving very little energy within yourself.

"Where your attention goes, energy flows. And where energy flows, whatever you're focusing on grows."

— Tony Robbins

Without boundaries, our attention and energy will continually focus on everything outside us. Every time we say yes to something that does not feel aligned and expansive, we say no to our joy.

Bringing peace, love, inspiration, creativity, and happiness back into your life begins by setting boundaries, so your energy stays within you.

Do not mistake this for selfishness.

Setting boundaries is not a selfish act that puts your needs before the needs of others, but an act of mindful love that recognizes that your needs are just as important as the needs of those around you.

It is an act of courage that allows you to make space for yourself and prioritize your mental, physical, emotional, and spiritual well-being — something most are too afraid to do.

Boundaries are part of taking care of yourself, showing yourself respect, and honoring your needs without disregarding those around you. In setting boundaries, you practice self-love and create a space to grow and flourish.

The best way to help the world is to help yourself first, not by sacrificing yourself.

A rising tide lifts all ships. You are the tide that can lift all other ships when you prioritize your own peace.

We can only give what we have, so if we sacrifice everything, including our peace and joy, for others, what do we have left to offer at the end of the day? Are we truly helping anyone if we do that?

Are we not of better service to others when we are full of peace, love, and joy ourselves?

When we are in these expansive states, our mere presence becomes an act of service.

Our state comes from our energy, and energy is infectious. Whatever state we are in can be felt by those around us and vice versa simply because of the emotion (**energy** in motion) we emit.

People are not inspired by what we say or do but by how we make them *feel*.

By giving ourselves what we need and prioritizing our peace, we not only take back our lives but also begin truly living and feeling alive. This expansive state you experience positively affects every other area of your life and the people around you.

We cannot change others, but by beginning to say yes to ourselves and what brings us peace, we inspire others to do the same for themselves.

One of the most effective ways to transform the world is not by telling others how to do it or doing things for them, but by being that change so unapologetically that it is impossible to ignore.

Setting boundaries is not a selfish act that puts your needs above others, but an act of mindful love that recognizes that your needs are just as important as the needs of those around you.

Chapter 3
How Boundaries Create Space for What You Want

Boundaries are created when we say no to what drains us of energy or no longer serves us. When we say no, we are creating space.

For there to be new creation, there must first be space. You cannot fill a cup that is already full. We must first empty our cup if we want anything new to come into our lives.

Boundaries are the medium through which we can create space for new possibilities.

Nature is fascinating. Whenever a void or vacuum (space) is created, nature has the tendency to quickly fill it with something. There need not be much effort to fill your life with beautiful things and feelings because the universe naturally fills up the space we create in our lives.

For instance, when was the last time you spent a whole day doing nothing when you had a day off? Whenever you have a free day, something always comes along to fill it, and I'm sure you did not have to try awfully hard to do that. This is nature at work, constantly filling up space where it is created.

Setting boundaries acts as a filter to prevent anything that no longer brings us energy and joy from entering our lives. Our job is not to force positive things to happen but to create enough space (through boundaries) to allow the new experiences we want to fill our lives naturally.

You can compare this to fishing in a river. You do not need effort to move the river. It moves on its own, but you need the right net to catch the things you want. Boundaries are the net you cast that allows you to catch what feeds your soul and filter out what no longer serves you in the river of life.

Most of us do not even have a net in the river and expect the river to throw what we want up onto the shore for us. The river is not the problem. Our way of interacting with the river is.

Boundaries are the net you cast that allows you to catch what feeds your soul and filter out what no longer serves you in the river of life.

Chapter 4
How to Set Boundaries
(Exercise)

I will no longer feel guilty for saying ‘no’ and for giving my body, mind, and soul what it needs.

Become acutely aware of where your energy is going in your life. What feels heavy? What is draining? What leaves you feeling depleted? How would you feel if you no longer had to do those things that leave you feeling this way? Be as specific as you can. The more specific you are, the more powerful the effects of the boundary will be.

Sovereignty comes from boundaries. You have the power to set those boundaries that protect your energy. Every boundary you set is an act of self-liberation.

Your peace is not something you need to fight for but something you already have and must protect. We choose to give our peace away when we keep saying yes to what does not serve us.

Make a list of what drains your energy or robs you of your peace.

Then create a boundary in the form of a statement so that when you encounter a situation where you must decide what to do, you'll already have made the decision to protect your peace.

It helps to add a reason as to why you are creating this boundary. The reason will be the consequences you face if you do not set this boundary because pain motivates us much more than pleasure.

Write down what first comes to mind, and don't overthink it. Follow your intuition.

Here are examples of boundary statements:

- I will no longer eat/drink x because it makes me anxious and tired and leads me to make decisions that do not serve me or others around me.
- I will no longer consume x media because it makes me feel like I'm not enough.
- I will no longer participate in negative self-talk because it takes away my peace and joy.
- I will no longer stay in a negative environment where people judge, criticize, or gossip about me or others. If I am in an environment like that, I will leave.
- I will no longer feel guilty for saying 'no' for giving my body, mind, and soul what it needs.

Here's a template for creating your own boundary statement:

- I will no longer ________________ because it makes me ________________.
- I will no longer (*behavior you want to stop*) because it makes me (*consequence of the behavior*).
- Once you have written out your boundary statements, identify which consequence is the heaviest and most painful.
- Then pick the one boundary that would impact your life the most when you implement it.
- For maximum effectiveness and the highest chance of success, focus on this one boundary for the next month.

Write it down and keep it somewhere visible so you are constantly reminded of it. Whenever you encounter a situation that causes you to suffer, use the emotional pain to trigger your memory of the boundary and do everything in your power to honor it.

Become aware of how you feel when you are honoring your boundaries so you remember the reason you are enforcing them.

For the boundary to be effective, it is important to discover the root cause of why you feel the way you do. You'll know you've found the root cause when you create a boundary, and it solves the issue you are facing permanently. If the issue resurfaces even after honoring the boundary, then you will know you haven't set a boundary at the root cause but a symptomatic one.

Use the space below to write your own boundary statement that would have the most significant impact on your life right now:

Date:

Chapter 5
Protecting Your Peace: Communicating Boundaries

As you set boundaries, they will be stress-tested by life. There will be boundaries you set that trigger resistance in others, especially if they have attached their happiness to you doing something for or with them.

When asked to do something that oversteps a boundary, it is usually best to peacefully say 'no' without needing to explain further. Many times that will be enough, but sometimes it will not.

If you encounter a situation where someone is asking for further explanation, at this point, you can explain the boundary you have set from a place of love and empathy. View it as sharing your truth and why you needed to create this boundary for yourself.

Sharing why you have set a boundary makes no one right or wrong. It is simply what you need right now, and this is always subject to change in the future. Most people will understand when you genuinely share from your heart why you need the boundary you have set.

How others react is influenced by *how* we share something. The intention, energy, and emotion behind what we're saying have a powerful effect on how the message is received. If you share your boundary peacefully from a place of love, more times than not, you will have an interaction that reflects the state you are coming from.

This does not work in every single circumstance, and sometimes even when you are in a peaceful state sharing your boundaries from a place of love, explaining why you've done so and how important it is to your well-being, others will still be upset, frustrated, and angry with you.

If you have mindfully and peacefully shared your boundaries and this is still happening, know that this situation is more about the other person than you.

If this happens, you can choose to open up a conversation to explore what makes them feel this way and what makes it upsetting. Or, if it seems like nothing you say or do will help in that moment, you can reschedule the conversation for another time when you have both had some time to let things settle. The important part is that how you both feel is communicated and that it isn't ignored or swept under the rug. In relationships, solutions can only come from communication.

Boundaries bring change, and accepting change can take time for others. Most times, if you are setting boundaries from a place of self-love, any upsets will settle down quickly as people realize that your boundaries are more about you than them.

However, there may also be times when space and time will not fix things. This is often a reflection of the relationship or the state of the other person's boundaries (or lack of). You cannot expect those who do not love themselves enough to set and honor their boundaries to understand yours.

It is essential to know that you cannot control how people react to the boundaries you set in your life. There will always be people who disagree with your decisions, but ultimately it is your life, and it is your responsibility to create one that brings you peace, love, and joy — even if others do not understand it.

Our responsibility is to do our best to understand where others are coming from, why they feel the way they do, and create space for them to share what feels true to them.

In any relationship, you are either growing together or growing apart. As you grow, your boundaries will change, and the relationships that are no longer aligned may begin to grow apart. This is a natural result in relationships if you are each heading in different directions in life, and it's important to understand that it is okay.

It's okay to both cherish and grieve what you once had and to let go and let yourself grow. All we can do is our best and sometimes that isn't enough for others, but we must have the courage to understand that our best is enough for us to find peace. If the relationship is grounded in love and meant to be, the other person will understand that your peace is just as important as their happiness when you communicate what you need.

"'No' might make them angry, but it will make you free. If no one has ever told you, your freedom is more important than their anger."

—Nayyirah Waheed

Peace is found when we become okay with being misunderstood by others.

Chapter 6
The Power of Universal Application

When we learn something new and implement change, we tend to only apply the change to that one area of our lives.

Let's say we have the goal of wanting to feel better in our body. We may learn about a new diet and realize that some foods we eat make us feel lethargic and anxious, so we work hard to identify what those foods are and no longer eat them.

After a few weeks, we begin to feel healthier and better about our bodies. If we continue this habit because we see how beneficial it is for us, it may become a permanent behavior change for life.

Many of us will stop the momentum of self-transformation here because we have achieved our initial intention of wanting to feel better physically. But we do not realize we can take it a step further and apply what we've learned in this specific instance to other areas of our lives.

Every positive change contains a principle that can be applied to other areas of our lives. Doing this not only continues the momentum of change but compounds your efforts.

If we eliminated certain foods from our diet and experienced the positive effects on our mood, could we apply this same idea to what we consume in other areas of our lives?

Could what we put into our minds affect the way we feel?

What would happen if we audited the media we consumed and eliminated things that drain us of energy or make us more susceptible to negative emotions?

The principle we have extracted from feeling better on a food diet is that everything we consume influences us, including what we consume with our minds.

This now gives the saying "we are what we eat" a whole new meaning, especially if we change the expression to "we are what we consume" to make it more universally applicable.

There are infinite principles we can uncover from any particular experience. This was just one example.

From the same dieting situation, we can also realize that our inputs create our outputs. If we only focus on changing the output without changing the input, it is equivalent to treating the symptom, not the cause.

It would be difficult to lose weight by only trying to exercise instead of also looking at the inputs that have caused the weight to exist in the first place. Without changing the input of food while working on losing weight, our efforts to exercise would be futile.

The main principle I want to highlight here is that when you experience positive change in one area of your life, look for ways to apply it to other parts of your life you want to improve.

The examples above relate to this book because each scenario was an example of setting boundaries and the life-altering effects of doing so.

In the first example of the diet, we created a boundary on what we will no longer put into our bodies because we do not enjoy how we feel if we do. In the second example, we created a boundary around the media we consume for the same reason as the first.

To experience the true power and full potential of any change you make, look for the **universal application** of what you have learned. When you do this, there is no end to the transformation and growth you can experience. This is how you can begin the journey of mastering your life holistically.

Exercise:

- Potential Areas of Your Life to Create Boundaries for:
- Mind
- Emotional & Spiritual
- Family
- Social Relationships
- Work/Career

Here is an acronym that is helpful to remember when negative thinking shows up:

BARF

- **B - Breathe.** Take five deep belly breaths to calm your nervous system and ground you in the present.
- **A - Ask** yourself, "Is this negative thinking useful?" If not, let it go.
- **R - Remember** and repeat to yourself that "negative thinking is the root of emotional suffering."
- **F - Feel** whatever emotion you're experiencing without needing to judge or comment on it (don't think, just feel).

Repeat this process until you have calmed your nervous system and the negative thinking has passed.

You may think of it as 'BARFing' your negative thinking to help it leave your system.

Without perpetuating our emotions through negative thinking, it takes roughly 90 seconds for our body to process and regulate emotions. This is how long it can take for negative thinking and the feelings associated with it to pass when you set this boundary.

Reference this framework the next time you are confronted with negative thoughts, and repeat the process until you are calm. When you practice this, it becomes a habit and eventually becomes your way of being where it is second nature.

- Body
- Romance & Partnership
- Finances
- Fun/Creativity/Hobbies/Recreation

Begin implementing just one boundary in only one area of your life until you've built a habit out of it.

Implementing too many at a time makes it significantly more difficult to upkeep. The best results for long-term transformation come from starting small, creating a habit out of one boundary at a time, and then moving to another.

You're ready to move onto the next boundary once you feel like the current boundary is part of you without needing to think about it much or exert much effort to maintain it.

Do not forget about the power of compounding efforts over time.

If you implemented just one boundary a month, you would have 12 boundaries in multiple areas of your life by the end of the year. It is impossible that your life won't look radically different in the best possible way by then. It only takes one boundary to change your life.

Remember, what you focus on expands. Where energy flows, things grow.

While it is essential to create boundaries between yourself and the external world, the most important boundaries are the ones you create for your inner world — within your mind.

Hundreds of circumstances happen for us every day in the external world, but it is all filtered through our mind.

It is not what happens for us that creates our emotions, but how we think about what happened that creates how we feel.

If we do not have any boundaries for our own thinking, then our mind will default to our conditioning and survival, causing us to suffer emotionally from being in a state of constant fear and self-preservation.

When left to its own devices, the mind looks for every possible threat in the environment, judges everything it encounters, worries about the future, regrets the past, and puts us in a perpetual state of stress.

This non-stop judgment and negative chatter in our minds is the root of our suffering.

But this is only one part of the story, and you always have the power to change the narrative or, better yet, to let go of it entirely. You do not

have to keep reliving the same chapter over and over again. Setting a boundary is how you can close a chapter in your life and begin a new one.

You are one thought, one decision, one boundary away from living a completely new experience of life.

How would you feel without the negative voice in your head? What would your life look like? How much more peace, love, and joy would you experience?

A mind empty of negative thinking creates space for a life full of peace.

Once you decide you will no longer allow yourself to think negatively, the emotional effects of negative thinking are significantly reduced or even eliminated.

We only continue to think negatively and worry because we believe there is some benefit in doing so, but how often has that led to your peace and joy?

Asking yourself these hard questions is how you can reveal the truth behind how your current actions are no longer serving you, so you can let them go to create space for new ones that do.

The way to break the self-destructive cycle of negative thinking is to remind yourself that nothing good comes from it and that it only steals your serenity.

Each time a negative thought enters your mind, you have the choice of continuing the emotional pain or deciding to stop it because you no longer want to suffer.

This boundary you create within your mind will be one of the most impactful choices you can make for your peace, happiness, and fulfillment.

How to Practice Holding Your Boundary Against Negative Thinking

Upholding a boundary may not always be easy, but it is simple. Do not mistake simplicity for lack of effectiveness. More times than not, simplicity and effectiveness are directly correlated.

Maintaining this boundary is simply making the decision in real time to no longer give your time, energy, and attention to the negative thoughts that pop into your mind.

Remember, what you focus on expands. Where energy flows, things grow. If you continue to give negative thinking your attention, it will only magnify. When you decide to no longer give it your energy (life force), its intensity dissipates and it passes through you much more easily.

So when negative thoughts arise, acknowledge them for what they are, but know that you do not need to get involved or believe in them.

It helps to take a few deep breaths, stand your ground firmly, and remind yourself that you will not think negatively because nothing good comes from it, and it only leads to emotional suffering. This naturally creates space in your mind, and this space holds infinite possibilities for what you want to enter your life.

Here is an acronym that is helpful to remember when negative thinking shows up:

BARF

- **B - Breathe.** Take five deep belly breaths to calm your nervous system and ground you in the present.
- **A - Ask** yourself, "Is this negative thinking useful?" If not, let it go.
- **R - Remember** and repeat to yourself that "negative thinking is the root of emotional suffering."
- **F - Feel** whatever emotion you're experiencing without needing to judge or comment on it (don't think, just feel).

Repeat this process until you have calmed your nervous system and the negative thinking has passed.

You may think of it as 'BARFing' your negative thinking to help it leave your system.

Without perpetuating our emotions through negative thinking, it takes roughly 90 seconds for our body to process and regulate emotions. This is how long it can take for negative thinking and the feelings associated with it to pass when you set this boundary.

Reference this framework the next time you are confronted with negative thoughts, and repeat the process until you are calm. When you practice this, it becomes a habit and eventually becomes your way of being where it is second nature.

“Whatever you are willing to put up with is exactly what you will get.”

— Unknown

Chapter 7

The Most Important Boundary You Can Create

Chapter 8

Boundaries Breed Creativity: How You Can Have It All

When we set goals, we often get into the mindset of attaining them at all costs. This often leads to an imbalance in our lives, as we sacrifice everything, including ourselves, for the sake of achieving the goal.

We prioritize productivity and achievement at the expense of ourselves.

We fill our schedules with tasks and duties, leaving no space for joy or happiness. We become so engrossed in achieving that we forget who we are and what's truly important to us.

The problem with this approach is that it often leads to burnout, frustration, and a feeling of emptiness once the goal is achieved.

Is it true that we can only achieve all of our goals or have time for hobbies and what we love? Is it true that we can only attain all of our career goals or spend time with our family?

More times than not, we assume that we can only have one or the other when it is possible to have both.

We do not live in an "either-or" world but in an "and" world.

You can achieve all your goals AND have time for what you love. You can attain your career goals AND spend time with your family. We live in a world where you can do what you love AND make a living.

Without belief, there is no space for new thoughts to come into your mind, and you will continue to do what you have always done and, therefore, get what you've always gotten.

Once you believe you can have both desires or even consider it a possibility, you open the door for new ideas that can transmute what you want into reality.

Creating Boundaries that Help You Live in Alignment Where You Can Have It All

Instead of sacrificing everything to attain an arbitrary external goal that will most likely leave us feeling unfulfilled, a better and more sustainable approach is to create boundaries or constraints around how you achieve your goals where you can have it all.

There is never just one way to do anything or even a "right" way to do it, and this is especially true for creating and achieving goals.

For example, if your goal is to make more money, instead of striving to do it at all costs, create a boundary of wanting to achieve it by working less.

While we may want to make more money, we probably don't want to work 14 hours a day, seven days a week, sacrificing our family, happiness, and health to attain it.

Creating a boundary of working less forces us to think differently and become more creative with how we can make it possible. It helps us consider new alternatives we never thought of before. Boundaries are the door to creativity and will help you create space for a more balanced life where you can have the best of all worlds.

Knowing what boundaries to create with your goals helps you to think deeply about what gives you true fulfillment and joy in life.

What makes you feel expansive and alive? Is what you're doing right now making you feel that way?

When we set goals, we believe we will be happy after we achieve them, but how many goals have you achieved in your life that sustained the feeling of joy for longer than a few days?

More often than not, we quickly become unsatisfied and move on to the next goal, frantically pursuing it just to get another hit of fleeting satisfaction that lasts shorter than a car air freshener.

It doesn't have to be this way. It is entirely possible to be happy in the present moment and not delay our joy for the illusion of a goal that gives an empty promise of happiness after achieving it.

The way to do this is to create boundaries around your goals where you can design your joy into the process.

When creating your goals, think about what would make you feel expansive, alive, and fulfilled in the present.

What boundaries or criteria would allow you to create a life you love right now?

It may help to invert the process by thinking about what currently drains you of energy and joy and then designing a life you want from that perspective.

Do you want to spend more time with your family? Do you want to do what you love and make a living? Do you want to start a business? Do you want more time to enjoy your hobbies? Do you want to make more money? Do you want to work more or less for it?

Would more money really make you happier? Let's say you made twice as much as you do now. Would you be twice as happy? What would you do with the money? Would that bring you true happiness and fulfillment? What would make you genuinely fulfilled?

What would you do or create with more time? Could you begin doing some of that now, to any small degree? What ideas do you have that would allow you to do that?

There are no wrong answers and no "right" way to design your life, but it is important to ask yourself these hard questions to begin knowing what you truly want. No one else can tell you this.

Creating a life you love begins by knowing yourself.

If something feels like it is missing from your life, you are most likely missing a boundary that can create space for what you want. Use that feeling as a trigger to ask yourself what boundary you are missing that would support the life you desire, and then make the decision to implement the boundary.

Create boundaries around your goals where you can design your joy into the process.

Chapter 9
Letting Go & Creating New Boundaries

“Some of the bravest things you can do are to say ‘no’ and set boundaries when you spent a lifetime convinced that you needed to please others in order to be loved.”

— Xavier Dagba

Nothing in this world is absolute. The only constant is change. What doesn't grow and evolve dies. We are always growing and changing, but if our boundaries do not, we will be confined by the very mechanism that helped us get to where we are.

As much as boundaries can set us free, they can easily confine us if we are not aware.

For instance, we may have set a boundary where we will only go out with family or friends once a month to focus on our own healing, but if we have made significant progress in our healing and now have the desire to deepen our connection with others, then this boundary we have set will only hinder our growth.

As we grow, our priorities and desires shift. If we were diligently focused on our career and have created boundaries around that, but we have now started a family, our priorities may have altered, and our boundaries will need to support that evolution.

It's okay to let go of boundaries and create new ones. It is the natural process of life.

This doesn't make us fickle or undisciplined. It makes us conscious and aware of our true selves and the ever-changing reality of life. This is how we honor our humanity.

What got us here may not get us there. What once served us may no longer serve us.

This doesn't make any of our existing boundaries wrong; it just means we have outgrown the pot we were planted in.

Being aware of your evolving needs, priorities, and intentions will allow you to let go of the old and set new boundaries where they are needed to create the life you want in the present.

Let go of the boundaries restricting your growth, draining you of energy, or preventing you from expressing your true self.

Create new boundaries that support your expansion and make you feel alive and aligned with yourself.

“When I let go of who I am, I become who I might be.”

— Lao Tzu

Final Note

While this is the end of the book, it is the beginning of a new life for you.

Nothing changes unless you do.

Decide in your mind that this is the most important thing you can do for your peace and joy and that you do not want to suffer in the way you have been any longer.

The most impactful and transformative boundary to implement is to no longer think negatively.

Create this boundary for yourself beginning now, and keep it top-of-mind for at least one month. Make a promise to yourself that you will keep this boundary and become very aware of how you feel during the next week. You will begin to notice a whole new feeling and experience of life within a few days.

When you are struggling, refer back to the chapters relevant to your current situation. Thank you for allowing me to guide you and be part of your journey.

With All My Love,

Joseph

P.S. I do have one small favor to ask. If you have found this book helpful or insightful, it would be an incredible honor if you could take 60 seconds to leave a review on Amazon about this book.

I would truly love to hear your thoughts, insights, story, and everything in between. The few words you share there will help spread this message to so many souls who are also looking for the same answers you are, and it has the potential to change someone's life (because who doesn't read Amazon reviews before they buy something?)

Thank you from the bottom of my heart, and I wish you all the love in the world.

A Short Summary & Helpful Reminders

- Create your boundaries and honor them deeply. Honoring your boundaries is honoring yourself.
- Our boundaries are a reflection of what we value.
- Saying no is self-care.
- Normalize saying no without feeling guilty.
- It is not what happens for us that creates our emotions, but how we think about what happened that creates how we feel. Let go of your thinking to change how you feel.
- Meet resistance and everything in life with peace and love.
- The external world responds to how we feel internally.
- Boundaries set you free.
- Boundaries create space for what we want to enter our lives.
- A life of peace comes from knowing you cannot please everyone.
- You cannot control how others feel, but you can honor their emotions.
- It is not your responsibility to change how others feel. Peace is a choice each person must make for themselves.

"Daring to set boundaries is about having the courage to love ourselves even when we risk disappointing others."

— Brené Brown

- To experience the true power and full potential of any change you make, look for the **universal application** of what you have learned.
- Setting boundaries is not a selfish act that puts your needs above others but an act of mindful love that recognizes that your needs are just as important as those around you.
- You cannot expect those who do not love themselves enough to set and honor their boundaries to understand yours.
- Seek to understand yourself, and be okay with being misunderstood by others.
- If something feels like it is missing from your life, you are most likely missing a boundary that can create space for what you want. Use that feeling as a trigger to ask yourself what boundary you are missing that would support the life you desire, and then implement the boundary.

- Let go of the boundaries restricting your growth, draining you of energy, or preventing you from expressing your true self.
- Create new boundaries that support your expansion and make you feel alive and aligned with yourself.

For Those Interested In My Other Books

- Don't Believe Everything You Think: Why Your Thinking Is the Beginning & End of Suffering
- Beyond Thoughts: An Exploration of Who We Are Beyond Our Minds
- Healing Anxiety & Overthinking Journal & Workbook: Let Go of Anxiety, Overcome Fear, Find Peace & End Suffering
- The Couple's Connection Journal: 33 Questions to Create More Intimacy, Understanding & Love With Your Partner
- I also have courses on writing and creativity.
- You may find my work and connect with me on my website at www.josephnguyen.org. My books can also be found on Amazon and many other online sites that sell books.